HOW TO GET REALLY GOOD AT SPANISH

Learn Spanish to Fluency and Beyond

3rd Edition

POLYGLOT LANGUAGE LEARNING

TABLE OF CONTENTS

LEARN LIKE A POLYGLOT

W hen it comes to learning foreign languages, people want to learn fast. They want to save time. People want quick results, and they want to be able to speak fluently in a short amount of time.

But how long does it take to become fluent in Spanish? The answer depends on your definition of the word "fluent" as well as your personal goals. Are you looking to visit a Spanish speaking country and learn a handful of words and phrases before departing? Do you want to be able to hold a basic conversation with strangers in Spanish? Is your plan to work a job that requires Spanish proficiency at the professional level?

When you understand how to learn a language fast and effectively, you will be able to meet all of those goals and go even further than you had previously imagined. Faster language learning methods and techniques do exist, and they can help you get to your goals exponentially faster.

To find these techniques and strategies, polyglots or people who speak several languages can offer us some important insight. Interviews, news stories, and viral videos with millions of views make these people out to be language geniuses, but if we look more closely at their stories rather than their abilities, the real truth begins to surface. They often struggle intensely in learning their first foreign language, but something finally clicks within the gears of their minds. They learn that first one and go on to easily learn three, four, or even more.

Also, they mostly all ditched school as a primary means to learn a language. Foreign language classes teach you about specific languages, but they do not teach you how to actually get good at a foreign language. After lectures and lengthy explanations, you are left to your own study devices to review massive amounts of vocabulary and grammar so that they hopefully stick in your head.

We don't know any better as first time language learners, so we memorize vocabulary and phrase lists, do workbooks, reread old dialogues, and repeatedly listen to the same audio tracks found in our coursebook CDs. It can be extremely boring at times, but if you are studious enough, you will finish and graduate.

Even upon graduation, however, you will find that school alone does not train our minds to understand the wide variety of vocabulary, sentence structures, and seemingly blazing fast speed that native speakers use in real life. While classes do offer several benefits for a hefty fee, they aren't enough. To truly reach an advanced level in a foreign language, you will need to become an autodidactic (self-taught) learner.

The Language Learning Bubble

Most polyglots weren't always good at learning foreign languages. It's a skill that they develop with each new language they take on. This is why the first one can be such a challenge for everybody.

Without that language learning skill and experience, trying to learn and memorize thousands of Spanish words, phrases, and grammar structures can seem like the ultimate test. And then, native speakers spit all of this out at seemingly a bazillion words a minute. It certainly sounds like a lot of hard work and study will be needed.

It's hard to argue against the value of hard work. It creates high-quality results. It pushes people to do what they need to do. It gets things done. But in the case of learning a foreign language, hard work can be somewhat misleading.

Rereading, rewriting, and re-listening to the same vocabulary, sentences, dialogues, and short stories may work well enough to pass your school exams, but they are not very effective means to store new language in your long-term memory. They are also tedious and not very fun ways to learn.

These simple methods may put new words into your short-term memory, but if you hope to be a fluent Spanish speaker one day, you'll need to store these words into your long-term memory and be able to recall them with ease. You'll need to instantly recognize them whether they are written or spoken.

All of this is possible and relatively easy to achieve, but traditional learning and study is not how you get to this point. While some initial study is recommended to learn and acquire the basics of Spanish grammar including simple vocabulary and phrases, traditional learning and studying becomes less and less effective as the number of words and phrases you encounter increases.

Polyglots teach us that it is far more effective to learn and retain these thousands of words and phrases through extensively reading and listening to native materials. You get really good at Spanish or any language not by reviewing and mastering a few hundred pages of grammar rules and vocabulary lists but by reading thousands of pages and listening to thousands of hours of native Spanish.

Many language learners, however, do not freely read and listen to native materials, and it's easy to understand why. It's completely overwhelming in the beginner and intermediate levels. On a single page of anything written in native Spanish, you'll find more words that you don't know than words that you do know. And it's extremely difficult to listen to native Spanish for very long when you really can't understand anything that is going on.

Nothing is broken down nor explained in native materials, so it's very easy to understand why language learners gravitate towards mostly language learning materials. In traditional learning materials like coursebooks or classes for example, it's the exact opposite experience. Everything is broken down and explained so that is simple to digest and absorb.

While these instructional materials can be helpful especially in the beginner levels, the problem is that most language learners stay far too long within the bubble of these traditional learning methods and materials. They spend too much time memorizing and reviewing the few hundred or thousand words they have accumulated while native speakers use more than 30,000 words to communicate with each other in daily life.

The Crash and Burnout

A handful of hardcore Spanish learners out there may determine that they just need to study for three or more hours a day to achieve the results they desire. We understand this deep and burning desire to learn, and we have even previously identified ourselves with that level of studious effort. It might seem like we should spend three or more hours studying every day considering all of the phrasebooks, coursebooks, grammar books, flashcard programs, apps, and online tools available.

If you have ever reached the intermediate stages of a foreign language, however, you might have experienced the frustration in trying to manage all of this studying and reviewing. You forget words. You forget grammar rules that you have read multiple times. And of course, native speakers still talk too fast. It's quite easy to find yourself in language learning hell. Many dedicated Spanish learners simply burnout and quit before ever reaching fluency.

The truth, however, is that there is no need to study for three or more hours each day to achieve fluency. The real issue preventing many people from learning Spanish is their definition of what it means to learn a foreign language. This problematic definition is formed from being required to take unimaginative and uninspired foreign language classes in high school and college. The excessive focus on studying and reviewing to pass exams in the short-term completely overshadows the long-term benefits of extensive reading and listening.

In the beginner phase or at any level, it would be a huge mistake to exclude content made by native speakers for native speakers in the target language. We aren't talking about *good* and *educational* sources to learn conversational Spanish from. We mean content that is fun and deeply interesting to you. You can learn from native Spanish materials that are exciting like movies, TV shows, music, videos, books, and video games.

Unfortunately, because of the initial overwhelming difficulty, beginners to language learning often omit this content in favor of more traditional learning from materials like textbooks, online courses, and audio lessons.

The Fast and Fun Way to Learn

The real Spanish language and the real fun in learning it, however, lies outside the bubble of instructional materials. It can feel like there is a massive set of essential vocabulary that we absolutely must know before tackling these fun materials. And if we do not know them, we feel we aren't ready yet. That feeling, however, is sure to keep us trapped in the language learning bubble.

In learning any language, there is no point where we become ready for native-level materials. You just have to start.

So how do you learn from fun things like Spanish novelas and movies? Do you just press play and listen as much as possible? But when you understand so very little in the beginner and intermediate levels, it can feel like we aren't learning anything at all. So then, do you continually stop to look up each new word that you find? But looking up every single new word and grammar structure can be absolutely exhausting. And on top of that, how are you supposed to remember all of them?

It's very easy to give up trying to learn through native Spanish materials. It's common to find yourself surrounded by thousands of words and question their usefulness in everyday conversation. Why would we ever need to know words like "Golpe Alfa" (Alpha Strike) and "Prisión de Agua" (Aqua Prison) from video games when we should be learning practical things like "sacar la basura" (to take out the trash) and "entrevista de trabajo" (job interview)?

But the truth is that you can learn all of these words and retain them easily. This book will show you how to do just that. It offers a solution to make it much easier to learn from native Spanish materials. With this, you can learn from any source of native Spanish that you like! And when given enough sources of native Spanish and time, you will eventually come to instantly understand almost anything in Spanish. As a result, you will also gain a natural intuition of how to express your ideas in Spanish using the same range of vocabulary and sentence structures native speakers use in real life. In other words, you will speak fluently.

Of course, you can also practice communicating with native speakers and receiving corrections to fill in for some of these hours. Learning via output does have its advantages. It offers a unique learning experience through interaction with native speakers and receiving corrections from them. It can also be used to gauge your progress.

The decision on how much you should practice outputting Spanish will be left to you. Extroverted people, or people who gain energy from meeting and talking to other people, will find practicing speaking and writing Spanish much easier, but introverted people may see more disadvantages than advantages here.

The Solution

Once you understand how to easily learn from native Spanish materials, you will be able to immerse yourself more deeply in whatever material you choose to read and listen to on a daily basis. And when you enjoy the learning process as a whole, you'll be willing to put in the hours of reading and listening every single day and naturally make faster progress.

If you are aiming for just a conversational level of fluency that allows you to hold basic conversations with native Spanish speakers, you may not need to put in these multiple hours every day. But if you want to understand everything native speakers say to each other and reach a truly high level of Spanish especially within a few years, you'll need to put in the hours of reading and listening each and every day.

Each chapter of this book will cover powerful language learning techniques and gradually expand on the overall main approach this book offers, but for now, here is a brief summary of that approach. Immerse yourself in any kind of native Spanish material of your choice without English subtitles or translations for roughly 20 minutes or so. This can include reading up on topics that you are highly interested in, watching exciting Spanish shows and movies, listening to your favorite music in Spanish, or even playing video games in Spanish.

For this brief amount of time, very carefully listen and look for words unknown to you and that are repeated multiple times. Without stopping the reading, video, or audio, quickly jot down the unknown words that are repeated two or more times. Include the page numbers, video times, audio track times, or in-game screenshots for reference later.

After the 20 minutes or so have passed, use online dictionaries and grammar resources to quickly break down the words and lines to learn their meaning. This will be easier to do with written materials, and some effort may be required to find video materials with transcriptions and subtitles in Spanish.

After fully learning these words and lines, pick up to two of them to create very specific reading, writing, listening, and speaking practice exercises using a free program called Anki (*www.ankisrs.net*). These exercises will help you practice and never forget both the lines you select and the more practical example sentences you find in instructional materials and grammar resources. As an alternative, you may use the Goldlist method to practice these lines and example sentences.

As you consistently mine a particular series, topic, or genre and regularly do these exercises, you will come to understand more of it very fast. You'll be actively searching for the high frequency words and learning them. These words are the key to slowly understanding what everyone is saying and what the main idea is. And the Anki exercises help to build up your confidence by making your progress more pronounced and visible.

Even if you are in the beginning stages of learning Spanish, this technique is highly recommended as you progress through learning the basics of the language. Reading, breaking down, and learning from native materials like videos, websites, and video games will be difficult at first, but early attempts to learn from these materials will immediately connect you to the real language used by native Spanish speakers every day. This connection will be sure to bring you excitement. It will also help build an early habit of freely reading, listening to, and watching native Spanish materials without English.

We invite you to experiment with these language learning strategies and see what brings you the most benefit and enjoyment in your personal journey to learn Spanish. We also hope you enjoy this book and find it helpful in simplifying the language learning process.

STARTING FROM ZERO

Early attempts to learn from native Spanish materials like novelas are most definitely encouraged for beginners, but without learning the basics of Spanish as you progress, your comprehension and language ability will be somewhat limited. Supplementing your learning with just a few basic Spanish grammar lessons can greatly speed up your ability to break down and understand language used by native speakers. This includes the ability to distinguish between formal, polite, and casual speech. Also, learning a bit about Spanish phonetics and practicing proper pronunciation from the very start will make it much easier for native speakers to understand you.

This chapter will attempt to provide a brief glimpse into the uses and limitations of language learning materials. You will also find a collection of advice you might find useful as a beginner or if you are currently working your way through a Spanish language course or book at any level.

There are so many ways to learn the basics to any foreign language these days, and we don't wish to dictate an exact process of how to get started. That should be your choice.

Start with whatever excites you the most! A few people will study only phonetics at first for months with the goal of sounding as native-like as possible. Some may be looking for more immediate results and will dive straight into communicating with native Spanish speakers on day one. Others may be looking for a more guided approach, so they start with websites and apps like Duolingo.

In the age of technology, quick internet searches, and YouTube, it is possible to learn anything including a foreign language without classroom instruction or even a single textbook. For the sake of streamlined learning, however, we would recommend a coursebook or textbook but a maximum of just one. A high-quality coursebook does provide well-rounded introductions to any foreign language. These introductions include solid grammar explanations and a wealth of easy-to-digest words, phrases, and sentences to start with.

Coursebooks and other Spanish learning resources provide a safe and sheltered source for learning, yet it is important to escape this language learning bubble as early as possible. Outside of that is where the true language and culture lie. There may be a set of two, three, four, or more coursebooks to learn Spanish, but you may only need the first one before you are able to learn solely from material made for native speakers. A habit of immersing yourself in native Spanish materials every day starting from day one can make that happen easily.

Taking Steps Every Single Day

Studying Spanish three times a week for 30 minutes will deliver mediocre results. By limiting yourself to such a small amount of time per week, you will struggle to understand and communicate in Spanish for 20 years before you are able to reach any level of fluency.

Languages are not just knowledge but also a set of skills our eyes, ears, mouths, hands, and brains must practice daily in order to achieve fluency. If you can only make 30 minutes to learn Spanish on your most chaotic days, so be it. You may not learn much for that day, but these small yet consistent actions do build towards new habits that will enable you to make this major lifestyle change.

Creating and maintaining this daily habit of learning Spanish will be one of your first challenges. Focus on not breaking the daily language learning habit at all costs. Consistency builds habits. Once that consistency and priority in learning Spanish has been established, you can build upon your daily routine by incorporating more learning activities like reading and listening to native Spanish.

This habit should not be taken lightly if you truly want to reach a high level of Spanish. You're trying to learn an entirely new foreign language and culture. If you want to be able to communicate in Spanish as well as you can in your native language, it's time to start taking things seriously. Show up every single day and learn what you can.

Phonetic Awareness

Regardless of whatever material you choose to begin learning with, incorporating phonetics early on in your program is highly recommended. Learning to speak with correct pronunciation should be a part of every program to master the Spanish language or any other language. Spanish phonetic knowledge and training will make your speech much easier for native speakers to fully comprehend. And they will notice the hard work you put into not just being able to communicate with them but also sounding similar to them. That is sure to make conversations much more comfortable and pleasant.

When practicing pronunciation, repeating words after a native speaker and attempting to mimic them is generally good practice, but without phonetic awareness and training, you are likely to still speak with a rather thick accent. When we learn to speak in new languages, we unconsciously and unknowingly project and apply the phonetic rules from our first language. We are hardwired to the speech patterns of our native language after speaking it for so long.

As a result, there are sounds in Spanish that you might not be able to recognize by ear and thus be unable to mimic without some basic phonetic awareness and training. Unfortunately, some Spanish language learners decide to skip this step without realizing its true importance, and the consequences of this decision can be found in their speech. For example, their vowel sounds may be too long. In comparison to their English counterparts, Spanish vowels are much shorter.

The good news is that this knowledge and training is easy to obtain and master with a little time and effort. It's as easy as studying the sounds of Spanish consonants and vowels and consistent practice. Anki exercises, listening to native Spanish materials, or even occasionally reading aloud offer such training methods.

The International Phonetic Alphabet (IPA) symbols may be new to you if you have never studied phonetics before. It can be a little overwhelming when looking at the entire IPA system, yet there is no need to study each individual letter and diacritic. You will only need to learn the symbols for the new sounds in Spanish and a few in English that will help you to make these new sounds. These symbols and their sounds will become familiar to you in just a few short days or weeks of practice.

The Sounds of Spanish

Our written explanation is meant only as a brief introduction to Spanish phonetics so that you are more aware of how to produce the new sounds with your mouth and tongue. You can find a free recording of a native Spanish speaker saying any word discussed in this chapter or virtually any Spanish word at Forvo (*https://forvo.com*). The next few sections can be initially challenging and possibly overwhelming at first glance, so we recommend grabbing a cup of coffee or two as you work your way through.

Many Spanish learners might pronounce "agua" (water) as "agwa", but it's actually "aɣwa". This [ɣ] sound is not found in modern day English. When we make the hard 'g' sound (the 'g' in "Gary"), we place the back of our tongue on the top of our mouths tightly and even temporarily restrict air flow. To make this [ɣ] sound, it's similar to saying the hard 'g', but the back of our tongue only gently touches the top of our mouth.

The 'd' in Spanish is also commonly overlooked by Spanish learners. The hard 'd' in Spanish like in "dar" (to give) is somewhat close to the hard 'd' in English like in the name "Dan", yet it is softer. To make this sound in Spanish, the tongue touches the back of the teeth rather than the gums. This small change makes a dramatic difference in accent reduction.

The soft 'd' in Spanish found in words like "puedo" (can I / may I) is even softer. This [ð] sound is so soft that it can sound more like a 'th' rather than 'd'. Make sure to pronounce "puedo" as "pweðo" rather than the gringo version "pwedo".

The letter 'll' found in words like "caballo" (horse) can be pronounced in many different ways depending on the region, but [ʝ] is its most common pronunciation. The [ʝ] sound does not exist in English, but it lies somewhere between the English 'y' like in "your" and the 'j' like in "jelly". It will take a bit of practice to get used to. This includes listening practice, as native speakers can jump from the 'y' sound to the 'j' sound when saying words containing 'll'. This also includes the 'sh' and [ʒ] (like the 's' in treasure) sounds spoken by native speakers from Argentina and Uruguay.

The infamous Spanish trilling 'R' [r] (alveolar trill) in words like "guerra" (war) is a common complaint amongst native English speakers learning Spanish and other foreign languages, but such complaints will bring you no closer to perfect pronunciation. They are a waste of your time and energy. Resolve to conquer the Spanish 'R' today.

There are hundreds of tricks to learn how to make this sound, but perhaps one of the simpler methods can be found in the English words "butter", "ladder, and "putter-up". The "tt" and "dd" sounds in these words require the [ɾ] (alveolar tap) which you already know how to do. This single roll or flap of the tongue is not a trill, yet it places your tongue exactly where it needs to be to produce one.

Practice playing around with these words at various speeds and see if you can get your tongue to flap or roll multiple times in the process. Success may be instant, or it may require a few days or weeks. If you practice daily and consistently, the trill will come to you without fail.

Let's quickly go through some other pronunciation mistakes that non-native Spanish speakers may not pick up on. The Spanish 'p' and 't' like in "pato" (duck) and "tortuga" (turtle) have no puffs of air like the English 'p' and 't'. The 'h' in Spanish like in "helado" (ice cream) is always silent. And the letter 'j' in Spanish is not all that unfamiliar if you can imagine someone from Scotland pronouncing the word "loch". If you can say the 'ch' in "loch", you can say this [x] sound found in words like "jefe" (boss).

Stress and Linking

While mastering the new consonant and vowel sounds and learning basic vocabulary, you may notice that all Spanish words are stressed at certain syllables. This is a feature found in English as well where the volume of certain syllables is increased. This concept should be somewhat easier to learn and master compared to training your tongue to produce completely new sounds. In fact, there are two rules to help simplify things.

If a word ends with a vowel, 'n', or 's', the stress goes on the next to last syllable. Examples of this first rule include "in-te-li-GEN-te" (smart) and "PI-co" (peak).

And rule number two says that if the word ends in a consonant other than 'n' or 's', the stress goes on the last syllable. Examples of this second rule include "to-MAR" (to take, to drink) and "ca-pi-TAL" (capital).

Whenever these rules are broken, an accent mark is used (á, é, í, ó, ú) which will tell where the correct emphasis needs to be placed. For example, "ES-ta" means 'this' but "es-TÁ" means 'it is'. As you can see here, stressing different syllables can completely change the meaning of a word. These accents can also distinguish words that sound the same but have different meanings like "tu" (your) and "tú" (you).

Linking words in Spanish is also vital to producing and understanding native Spanish. If the last letter of a word is the same as as the first letter of the next word, they blend together to make a single sound. This can be heard when "donde está" (where is it) becomes "don-des-tá" and "para alcanzar" (to reach) becomes "pa-ral-can-zar". Linking is also very noticeable when a word ends with a consonant and the next word starts with a vowel. This can be heard when "el amigo" (friend) becomes "e-la-mi-go" and "mis obras" (my works) becomes "mi-sob-ras".

It's highly recommended to listen to all of the individual sounds discussed in this chapter to gather a more complete understanding that our written explanation cannot provide. Perhaps one of the better demonstrations of Latin American Spanish pronunciation online can be found at *https://www.youtube.com/watch?v=XW1JADx5KP0*. This video can also be found by searching YouTube for "Spanish Latin American Pronunciation Video 1: The Spanish Consonants". The first video in that series handles the consonants. The second video teaches the vowels. And the third video is optional.

And if you would like to watch the equivalent video series for Castilian Spanish, you can find that at *https://www.youtube.com/watch?v=MOJG7Th2IpA*. You can also find this video by searching YouTube for "European Spanish Pronunciation, Video 1. Spanish Phonetics and Spelling".

If you are not a beginner but were unaware of some of these phonetic rules, there is no need to worry. You can always rewrite any unnatural speaking habits in Spanish that you may have developed thus far. This new phonetic awareness will slowly shape your pronunciation over time when paired with deliberate practice. Some learners even go as far as to record themselves to compare with a native speaker or to check on their progress from time to time.

Spanish Dialects

Of course, pronunciation and also a considerable amount of vocabulary change depending on which country you go to. Castilian (Spain) and Latin American Spanish follow a similar phonetic system but with significant differences. Most notably, there are the distinción, seseo, and ceceo dialects.

Castilian Spanish uses distinción (distinction) which uses both the [s] and [θ] (like the 'th' in 'thunder') phonemes (sounds). Essentially, words with 's' are pronounced with [s] (like the 's' in cups, hats, and books), and words with 'z' or with 'c' (before 'e' or 'i') are pronounced with [θ]. The word "distinción" itself would be pronounced similar to 'distinthión'. This is why people from Spain appear to speak with a lisp.

Nearly all Latin American countries and peoples follow the seseo dialect. The dialect is also found in small parts of the Andalusia region in Spain and the Canary Islands. In this dialect, words with 's' are pronounced with [s] and words with 'z' or with 'c' (before 'e' or 'i') are pronounced with [s] as well. As an example, "la casa" (the house) and "la caza" (the hunt) would both be pronounced as 'la casa' in Latin American Spanish. In Castilian Spanish, "la casa" would be spoken as 'la casa', but "la caza" would be said as 'la catha'.

The highly uncommon ceceo dialect can also be found in the Andalusia region on the Southern tip of Spain. In this rare rural dialect, the [s] and [θ] are both pronounced with [s̄] (a soft and fuzzy version of 'th'). Rather than imagining what a soft and fuzzy 'th' sounds like, your time might be much better spent by focusing on one of the two much more prominent dialects.

Luckily, a standardized Spanish language does exist, and learning it will allow you to start speaking with almost any native Spanish speaker in the world with some exceptions which we will discuss briefly. This standardized Spanish that is taught in online courses, coursebooks, and other language learning resources may lean towards Latin American Spanish and the seseo dialect, but it may or may not lean towards any specific country's dialect and vocabulary. It is advised that you check each language learning resource to see if it caters towards any particular country.

Every Spanish speaking country comes with multiple dialects that can seem like entirely new languages. This is because of the large extent that vocabulary and slang changes from country to country in the Spanish speaking world. For example, if you travel throughout the Caribbean and speak Spanish after exposing yourself to just the standardized version, there are going to be hundreds of communication issues between all the variations of Spanish you encounter.

If you have a specific country that you plan on traveling to or a specific nationality of people in mind that you wish to communicate with, you may want to start learning its region-specific vocabulary and dialect as you progress in learning standardized Spanish. This is especially true in the case of going abroad. Exposing yourself to just standardized Spanish is going to limit to a great extent your ability to comprehend and communicate with other people while living and traveling overseas.

These regional differences are not so much different than English, however. If you grow up in an English speaking country, you can travel to any other English speaking country in the world and still be able to communicate with almost anyone. You may need to learn a few new words to prevent any future confusion or misunderstandings, but everyone will be able to understand you regardless of your dialect. Although fully understanding all the local slang is another matter entirely.

That's Too Many Rules!

All of these pronunciation rules and dialects can be quite overwhelming, but there's no need to review and memorize all of this information like you would cram for a school test. Because you are now more aware of the phonetics of Spanish, you'll slowly start to notice these new sounds more and more when listening to native Spanish speakers. You will begin to build a natural intuition for how to pronounce words and gradually incorporate this information into your spoken Spanish. You can always refer back to the rules whenever you are confused about anything.

Spanish pronunciation is just one small example of how potentially easy it is to get lost trying to study and review large lists of rules and information in an effort to memorize them all. The way you get better at these rules, however, is not to memorize the rules at all. It's to practice them subconsciously by reading and listening to native Spanish as much as possible every single day.

By covering the basics of Spanish pronunciation, we hope we have provided a short but sufficient demonstration of the uses and limitations of language learning materials. We attempted to condense the phonetics of Spanish down to the most important points, and we could easily continue this discussion by getting into more complex topics such as vowel reduction and aspirated consonants. But at a certain point such as this, the advanced rules like these are more effectively learned through intuition and large amounts of input just like how native speakers learn. So, instead of studying rule by rule, learn it naturally word by word.

This same principle applies to the grammar lessons contained within your grammar course or coursebook.

Stop Taking Textbooks So Seriously!

Your textbook should be your loyal and faithful servant and not the other way around. Do not let it become your master. What we mean is that it should not take up the majority of your study and learning time.

Let these books briefly serve you, and then, dismiss them. Don't bother with drills and grammatical exercises if they don't interest you. Don't bore yourself with the comprehension questions in the book. Don't write out words over and over. Don't memorize verb conjugation tables and declension charts.

Understand the gist and get out of there! Seek just five minute explanations for new language and grammar structures. A daily habit of reading and listening to native Spanish materials as well as Anki will make sure that you receive more than enough practice.

Use your coursebook time to feed Anki the new information that you wish to practice. New vocabulary words, phrases, grammar structures, verb conjugations, monologues, dialogues, and long passages can be divided and conquered through a variety of Anki flashcard exercises. How to do so will be covered in Chapter Four.

It's not necessary to turn every new word and verb conjugation into an Anki card, or otherwise, you might fall asleep before you make it to the next chapter! Do what you can until you get bored and then simply move on. While coursebooks and Anki are helpful tools, they are not as nearly important as reading and listening to native Spanish materials.

A Most Common Mistake

Here's where beginning language learners make the most common mistake. It's a mistake that often puts an early end to many hopeful newcomers in learning a new language. There is no need to finish your initial course or coursebook before you try learning directly from native Spanish materials. You don't even need to finish the book or course at all! Learn what you can from it until you get bored.

Boredom is our brain's way of telling us that we are going to burn out if we continue to push ourselves to learn day after day from material we are not truly engaged in. Our brains are smart that way. They know when something is no longer working. Resistance to learning doesn't mean that we are stupid or lazy. It means to stop and do something different.

It's so easy to blame yourself for getting bored because you might feel that you should learn all this serious material before you get to learn from fun materials like Spanish movies and TV shows. That line of thinking, however, is not true at all. Learning directly from fun materials is the key to never getting bored and quitting.

Change materials whenever you find yourself continually getting bored and unable to focus. Jump between your coursebook and your true interests in the Spanish language. Whatever you truly desire to learn from is where you should go next. Listening to and following that desire is what keeps you learning. That's the secret to wanting to learn and improve each and every day.

Try to learn directly from native materials as soon as possible. When you personally make the connection between what you are learning from Spanish learning materials to what you see and hear in native materials, that will boost your motivation more than almost anything else. That is how you can eventually conquer all the serious Spanish you feel that you should learn.

Early Output or No?

The choice of whether or not to include output and communication with native speakers early on in the language learning process will be left to you. This is somewhat of a hot topic currently being debated within the language learning community and is worthy of its own book, but here is a summary of the main issue boiled down into a single sentence. Early output offers a unique way to learn through experimentation and corrections, yet at the same time, we run the risk of building unnatural speaking habits early on since it's difficult for native speakers to correct every single one of our mistakes.

Ultimately, you must decide when exactly to begin incorporating output practice. If you are seeking immediate results and would like to communicate with native Spanish speakers as soon as possible, speaking and writing in Spanish every single day becomes a natural priority. Some polyglots go as far as to speak with tutors from day one in only the target language, and others have demonstrated amazing results using input-only based approaches. Either way, we will discuss how to get into contact with native speakers and receive corrections in the last chapter.

How About More Advanced Textbooks?

You might feel that you haven't mastered the basics after one textbook, and this feeling may definitely reflect some truth. What about the everyday things in life in Spanish speaking countries: paying bills, renting an apartment, going to the bank, and working at a company? If you would like to live and work abroad one day, a certain set of vocabulary and phrases is going to be needed. You may even wish to purchase an additional coursebook to make sure that you don't sound like another helpless gringo. Go for it.

Some dedicated language learners find a series of coursebooks and textbooks to be interesting because progression and the learning process itself can be exciting. Every chapter brings new grammar structures that allow the learner to understand and express larger and larger ideas. The beginning months can be highly stimulating and intriguing since everything is new, and coursebooks present these new ideas and grammar structures in a way that is easy to understand.

Some of those who have reached the intermediate stages of learning a foreign language, however, can testify to what eventually follows after the first few textbooks are completed. We realize that we still struggle to understand most native material, so we buy more advanced books covering more grammar, phrases, and idioms. We go harder in our learning routine and study for more than three hours per day. These advanced grammar explanations are now long-winded, and new language can be highly situational. And there's always more vocabulary to study and review. The first few thousand came easy with some effort, but now suddenly there's 30,000 that we feel that we are expected to continually review!

It's so easy to become trapped and confined within a bubble of language learning materials. Learning can unknowingly become stale, boring, and inefficient for months and years. "Fun? There's no time for that. I have to study more!", may be the last words of your motivation before it disappears.

This book exists to say that you will have a lot more fun and motivation in the long-term when you supplement what you learn from fun things with these language learning materials. Of course, common sense says to do things the other way around. Then again, you have millions of hopeful people who begin learning Spanish and then drop out when things become too dry and boring.

An Alternative Course

Try using these advanced resources as just references to look up any new or unfamiliar language structures you repeatedly encounter in native Spanish materials. Wouldn't it be nice to quickly drop in, understand the gist of the target word or grammar structure, and be done with these resources? Lengthy grammar explanations can easily be forgotten, yet new words and grammar structures in the context of a story that you truly care about can burn in your memory for years. That's the power of context.

You might not even need any advanced Spanish textbook. In the age of the internet, quick searches to many questions can provide an accurate answer in just a minute or two. Online dictionaries can provide the basic meaning to an overwhelming majority of words and phrases and give plenty of example sentences. If more explanation is desired, internet searches for target sentence structures will reveal resources that can provide sufficient explanations to most structures.

LEARN FROM WHAT YOU LOVE

There is no point in time where you become ready for material made by native speakers for native speakers. It is certainly not when you complete that set of six Spanish textbooks. This imaginary point in time where you will magically be ready to understand everything doesn't exist. But the truth is that you don't even need to understand half of everything. You just need some simple rules which you will find in this chapter.

If you really want to reach an advanced level of Spanish within a few years, it is absolutely necessary to read, listen, and watch native Spanish materials for multiple hours every day. Although if your goals aren't set on reaching a high level of Spanish in such a short time frame, start with however much time you can commit to every day.

Doing more than 90 minutes or so every day of coursebook study and Anki review, however, is not recommended. When strict study time begins to exceed this amount of time, you'll begin to run into problems similar to those mentioned in the last two chapters. For that reason, after this strict study period ends, we encourage reading, listening, watching, and learning from native Spanish materials for as much as possible every day.

The 20-Minute Rule

Video games, comics, books, websites, movies, and TV programs all contain everyday Spanish that you can break down and learn from. If you have ever tried to study any of these materials diligently in the past, however, you know how enormous a task it can be. How do you focus long enough to break down an entire online article or even a short story line by line? How do you not become overwhelmed by websites where everything is in Spanish? How can you study a TV drama?

How do you keep up the willpower to continue these unsustainable study routines after just two days? The problem gets worse and worse. You can burn all of your initial motivation pushing yourself to break down and learn massive amounts of language until the day comes when you would rather do anything but another day of routine study.

Let's now revisit the method discussed in the first chapter but this time go into more detail. Immerse yourself in any native Spanish material of your choosing without English subtitles or translations for roughly 20 minutes. As you carefully read, watch, and listen, be on the lookout for the unknown words that you have seen or heard multiple times. Quickly write down the unknown words that are repeated two or more times and continue without stopping the reading, video, or audio. Include the page numbers, video times, audio track times, and screenshots for reference later.

In the case of reading native Spanish materials, you may use a dictionary to look up as many words as you need. Unlike video and audio materials, there's much less context to keep you engaged when there is just text and especially when there are quite a lot of words you don't know.

After the 20 minutes or so have passed, stop and examine your list of repeated words. Break down and learn the meaning of these words and the lines that they are found in by using online dictionaries and grammar resources. Once you have learned the meaning behind these high frequency words and their respective lines, pick zero, one, or two of what you feel are the most important passages to practice using Anki. For the purposes of this book, one passage can be a single long sentence, a few sentences, or even brief dialogues.

The Power of Context

But why pick just one or two passages to practice using Anki and not three or more passages? There are two main reasons behind this choice. First, the process of creating the Anki cards for just one or two passages already takes a significant amount of time and work. And second, it is to set a strict limit on how much you review through Anki.

Ideally, you want to spend minimal time with Anki so that you can make more time for more reading and listening to native Spanish. And with the help of the 20-Minute Rule, you can easily create more digestible lists of words and contexts to learn from.

Encountering new words, phrases, and grammar points from multiple contexts is how we build upon our understanding of how to use them. It also makes them harder to forget each time we encounter them.

For this reason, you can even pick zero passages to practice with Anki to go straight back to reading and listening. You may want to save Anki for the toughest words and grammar points that you have looked up over and over and still have trouble understanding. Using Anki or even the Goldlist Method to review every single new word or phrase you have learned can severely slow down the time it takes you to reach fluency.

There is an amazing process that slowly blooms as you read, listen to, and mine a single source of native Spanish for vocabulary and sentences. When you mine passages over and over from a particular subject matter for days and weeks, you will come to know its most commonly used words and phrases. Once you have a strong grasp on the high frequency words, you will be able to piece together more and more of the meaning of new content from that source as you first hear or see it.

When new words and phrases come from a much larger story or plot that you are highly interested in, all that new information becomes so much more memorable. Almost every line has character to it, and they can become unforgettable. It's the power of context.

Forget the Rest!

There is no need to translate entire drama episodes or online articles. Learning everything on your high frequency word list should be a large enough chunk of work as is. But if you feel you can handle more, by all means go through as many lines or sentences as you can before mental fatigue eventually surfaces. That fatigue signals that it's time to take a quick mental break before moving on to new content.

Watch videos and read materials just once and no more. Don't watch the same video, movie, or TV episode over and over until you break down everything from it for the sake of learning. That's no fun at all. What might be more fun is exploring the near endless amount of native Spanish material available online. Learning just a handful of lines of dialogue from each episode or chapter is enough to move on to the next.

That last line is so vital to making all of this learning fun, so we would like to repeat it. Learning just a handful of words or lines of dialogue from each episode or chapter is enough to move on to the next.

Spanish Is Not Too Fast

Using English subtitles to watch Spanish TV shows, movies, dramas, and videos is an English reading activity with some background noise. You will learn nothing outside a few basic words. You might be tempted to use them to help you focus on the story or relax after an intense study session, but if you choose to use them, native Spanish speakers will always talk too fast for you.

They will always talk too fast unless you take the time each and every day to practice trying to comprehend what they mean. But how can you comprehend them in the beginner and intermediate stages when they use thousands of words that you don't know yet? To answer this question, you must see listening comprehension as a skill. It's a skill that is built through practicing with whatever vocabulary that you do know at the time and relying on context for the words that you do not know.

You will understand the foreign language only by consistently trying to understand the foreign language. You need every chance that you can get to build towards your reading and listening comprehension. Some people like to cite that it takes roughly 10,000 hours of practice to achieve a high level of skill in anything, and this number may or may not be completely accurate. The value of consistent practice, however, is something most of us can agree on.

Listening comprehension is arguably the weakest skill of the average language learner, for they do not receive anywhere close to the amount of comprehensible input required to understand the spoken language as used by native speakers. While audio tracks accompanying language courses are certainly useful, you may quickly find that they do not provide the volume of practice necessary to understand native speakers out in the everyday world.

While subtitles in Spanish are extremely helpful to learning key moments from video materials, allow yourself to just listen for the full 20 minutes before delving into reading the subtitles. Sadly, these subtitles don't come equipped with the native speakers that you encounter in the real world, so think of it as practice in real-time.

Most of us don't have a family that can speak Spanish to us every day for 8-12 hours for 10+ years. You can pay tutors to do just that, but that becomes expensive to do every day for even just one hour a day. Without these adult native speakers constantly around, your ears remain incredibly weak. Listening to and reading native Spanish materials every day and regularly doing the Anki exercises will help to alleviate this problem.

No Subtitles, But How?

Train your ears to listen with your full attention and find the words that are both unknown to you and that are repeated frequently. The moments that you desire to understand the most can also be learned. Simply jot down the video times for later reference and don't press pause.

In case there are irremovable English subtitles in a video, you can block them from view by cutting out and placing a wide and thick but short piece of paper in front of your computer screen.

Keeping English subtitles out can be fairly difficult for some folks. You will be tested. You will need determination and faith to fight against the habit of doing everything in English. If allowed even for a brief moment, you feed the idea that you must understand everything to get the most enjoyment from the material.

This idea, however, is not necessarily true when you consider the enjoyment you gain as you gradually notice yourself being able to understand more and more Spanish each and every day. Seeing true progress in yourself is a feeling like no other. It is self-empowering.

Start by watching and reading things where the premise is easily understandable. You may want to first choose material that you have seen before, so you can get used to everything being in Spanish while still being able to follow the plot.

Despite how *good* it may be for listening practice, it can be maddening watching the same episode or movie five or more times within the same week. Watch and read how you normally would in your native language. Once is enough. And if you really enjoy the material, you can always revisit it just like you do in your native language.

Work towards building and maintaining a habit of freely listening and watching without stopping. Do not continually stop to look up words and phrases. Trying new material and getting lost quickly is frustrating, but when you do possess something that you personally find exciting and can understand the gist, that's where learning truly starts to take off. When you finally realize that you do not need to understand everything said and can still enjoy the material that you love, you will know victory.

Choose Easy

If you decide to practice and review one or two passages using Anki, let's make sure that they are appropriate for your level. If you select contexts with four or more unknown words altogether, it's still very much possible to break down all the vocabulary and grammar. Yet if you are repeatedly encountering these difficult passages from your high frequency word list, you may want to consider skipping a few of them. Too many new words, phrases, and grammar points can raise numerous questions to look up and make the learning process slow-paced and tedious.

These types of passages can lead to frustrating Anki exercises. When the difficulty level is set too high in Anki and also in general, it can cause your interest to wane and take the enjoyment out of learning and practicing Spanish.

Choosing easy can make learning Spanish so much more fun and even addictive. Choosing contexts with just one, two, or three new words allows learning to happen seemingly at a faster pace. When the level of the challenge before us is set at just the right level, we can enter a flow-like state where our learning becomes much more pleasurable and satisfying.

Double Check Your Work

Once you have broken down your high frequency word list and looked up the new vocabulary and grammatical information, you will have a far better understanding of the meaning of the context they came from. Understanding the exact meaning behind the words, however, can be tricky from time to time. It can be very easy to miss the underlying tone and hidden connotation in a foreign language, and this becomes more apparent whenever language is translated. Perhaps you have seen the results of this on photos of funny T-shirts or inappropriately translated signs in Asia. You wouldn't want something similar to happen to you when you spoke or wrote something in Spanish, right?

In that case, you should use the English subtitles and translations to double check the meaning of the words. Yet this doesn't mean that you should use English while first watching or reading native Spanish. After the 20 minutes or so of immersion time comes to an end, however, it is OK to check the English subtitles and translations to clarify any underlying tone and meaning of the words. It is highly important to make sure that you completely understand what you are trying to learn before you put it into practice. Language textbooks usually provide English translations for this reason.

All this subtitle and translation talk might sound somewhat contradictory, so here's an easier way to think about it. Native materials are for long and extensive reading and listening practice. Subtitles and translations are for short and intensive learning.

Where to Find Spanish Subtitles?

Obtaining the subtitles and transcripts for specific audio and video materials is not always possible. Yet once they are in your hands, learning straight from the material that you love becomes possible.

Perhaps the most readily available source of Spanish and English subtitles for TV shows and movies can be found on Netflix (*https://www.netflix.com*). The former days of desperately hunting down subtitles for days has come to an end, as Netflix offers Closed Captioning (CC) for virtually any Spanish TV show and movie in their library. In order to fully access these Spanish subtitles and even Spanish-dubbed materials, you will need to change Netflix's language settings to Spanish under "Account" and "My Profile".

Let's take a quick look at some other resources available that include Spanish subtitles. Univision on YouTube (*https://www.youtube.com/user/Univision*) offers a variety of content including clips from telenovelas, variety shows, sitcoms, news, films, and sports. And Telemundo's YouTube channel (*https://www.youtube.com/user/telemundotv*) offers a somewhat similar alternative.

If you are looking for something more inspirational and uplifting, TED Talks in Spanish can be found on YouTube as well by searching the site for "Ted Talks Español".

And if you are interested in news, politics, and foreign affairs, Euronews (*http://es.euronews.com*) provides news coverage in Spanish via video along with full transcripts.

Working Towards Immersion

The secret to being consistent in reading and listening to native Spanish every day lies in finding the Spanish hobbies that you truly care about. For example, if what you love to do is play video games in your free time, change the language settings to Spanish and don't look back. In fact, it may help to envision yourself as someone from a Spanish speaking country such as Spain. It may sound silly, but this kind of creative thinking will enable you to replace your old English hobbies one by one permanently.

Take the things you do in English that truly interest you and stir excitement from deep within and refuse to do them unless they are in Spanish instead. Advanced reading, listening, speaking, and writing skills will come as a natural result of spending thousands of hours living through the language.

Switch your primary source for learning to Spanish books, websites, music, or whatever got you interested in the language in the first place. Let this material become your new textbook. Learning from native Spanish materials that you truly love to read, watch, and listen to for fun makes it an absolute joy to put in those thousands of hours.

Foreign pop culture and TV do not have to be the end goal in learning a language. There is so much more to a language than what you might find on TV. Regardless of the language and culture, low-quality TV programs can numb the mind rather than excite it.

You will know exactly when you find the best native material for you to learn from. How? It will be addicting, and you won't want to put it down even after reading and listening to it all day.

This may require searching far and wide to find native Spanish materials that you genuinely care for, but we do this in our native language all the time. We try new things, and if we don't like them, we look elsewhere. So learn from everything you come across, and when you find yourself continually growing bored, move on to the next thing. There's literally an entire Spanish speaking world to explore.

Some folks may just wish to meet, befriend, and be proficient in communicating with people in Spanish. In this case, Facebook, Twitter, and other social media platforms provide instant gold mines of reading material to dissect.

You may also find new topics to read up on through social media. Press the "Like" button on Spanish pages and groups that pique your interest. Follow famous people that you admire. Immerse your social feed in only Spanish.

If what you truly enjoy is found mostly in reading, all the better. Reading has several advantages over listening, but we will cover these advantages in Chapter Five. In short, some of the world's most impressive polyglots like Alexander Arguelles and Luca Lampariello claim a strong habit of extensive reading is one of the secrets to their amazing language abilities.

And finally, going full immersion in your home environment is not required by any means, but it offers ample opportunities to get yourself used to relying less on English by reading and listening to more Spanish at all hours of the day. Some of these steps towards immersion you can immediately get used to, but others may take years in order to overwrite old habits that are strongly rooted in your native language.

Here are some ideas. Start your day by reading and watching the weather forecast for Spain in Spanish. Delete all songs in English from your music library and replace them with Spanish music. Change your computer and phone's language to Spanish. Use Spanish to learn a skill completely new to you like cooking a new dish for example.

SPACED RECALL SYSTEM

S imply encountering and looking up a new word or grammar structure does not mean that we have truly learned it. It may reside in our short-term memory for a short while, but we simply forget things as humans. If we can't recall a word while speaking or recognize it during a conversation, we haven't truly learned it yet. We acquire words and all of their connotations for good by encountering them over and over in a wide variety of contexts.

In general, rereading and rewriting new vocabulary, phrases, and sentences in mass is not very efficient in helping us retain that new information. It also happens to be incredibly boring and tedious.

Anki aims to simplify and consolidate our review time by combining intelligent flashcard exercises with a Spaced Repetition System (SRS). The SRS is designed to test us on information at intervals just before we are likely to forget. The Goldlist method is another way to review via the SRS.

While there are many benefits to these review systems, their main purpose is to help ease you into learning from native Spanish materials. The SRS offers a temporary solution to aid you in combating the initial high difficulty level of native materials. It assists your learning while you gradually build up your confidence to take on more and more native content.

We recommend using Anki only during the first three to six months of starting Spanish. After that point, if you have been reading and listening to native Spanish on a daily basis, you will no longer need to rely on the SRS. You will be used to immersing yourself in native Spanish content, and you'll be able to review more naturally what you learned through extensive reading and listening alone while making faster progress.

We believe what is most important about Anki is its ability to clearly measure and track the progress you have made in the beginning and early intermediate levels. At these levels, it's difficult to see visible and clear progress when reading and listening to native materials or when trying to express your exact thoughts with native speakers. In fact, it's very easy to get frustrated, and your efforts to learn here can feel like trying to drain a lake using only a single cup.

But with Anki, you can see clear and consistent progress in the amount of cards you make and in your ability to successfully recall things that you have learned. That feeling of clear and consistent progress helps you to keep learning especially on the days you really don't feel like it.

Some language learners out there hold a strong dislike for Anki and flashcards, and we can understand why. They can get really boring really fast. Flashcards can remind you of the useless facts that you were required to memorize for school tests and forgot just a week later.

Basic flashcards alone may be unable to hold your attention for very long, but that's the thing. It's just one amongst many review exercises. Problems can arise when you do nothing but basic flashcards in Anki. Additional problems begin to accumulate when you do excessive amounts of review, but we will cover that issue in the next chapter. First, let's just focus on the types of exercises themselves.

This chapter will introduce Production, Cloze, Listening, and Shadowing exercises in an attempt to make Anki a more viable option for more people by adding some spice and variety to traditional flashcards. These four exercise types will help you to practice any new vocabulary, phrases, and grammar that you wish to improve upon. When you combine these exercises in Anki, you get a single activity where you can practice reading, writing, speaking, and listening to Spanish all at once.

Anki does not come with any pre-made decks for Spanish or anything for that matter. Although you can download user-created decks for free, it's highly recommended by an overwhelming majority of the language learning community to create your own decks. Without that personal connection you get from making your own exercises using the material you are reading and listening to, you'll lose interest fast.

Your personal decks can be made using instructional materials, native Spanish materials, and also what you personally need the most help with. When you put the effort into creating the deck, the exercises come to life in a way. Combining these four exercise types alongside a wide variety of Spanish sources will help to keep you on your toes each review session. You will never know what is coming up next.

Production

Let's start with a very basic exercise but one with an important purpose. Simply, you'll be given a word in English or a picture and have to say aloud the equivalent word in Spanish. That's it. Yet it should not be underestimated because of its simplicity. When you have a strong mix and balance of other exercises to go with this simple one, this exercise is perfect.

Production exercises have two very important uses. First, our ability to speak a new language is greatly enhanced just by being able to recall thousands of very simple and straightforward words and phrases with lightning speed and little to no trouble. We need to know how to quickly say things like the following:

- azul (blue)

- círculo (circle)

- conductor de autobús (bus driver)

- cartón de leche (milk carton)

- tener dolor de garganta (to have a sore throat)

- lavar los platos (to wash the dishes)

- encender las luces (to turn on the lights)

- enchufar (to plug in).

That's where Production exercises in small quantities can help.

If you can't remember a word or phrase after five seconds, just retest it at a later time and move right along. Don't strain yourself in order to recall it. And don't try to push it into your mind in order to remember it next time. Those are short-term memory tactics. Some words and phrases require only a few tests to acquire while others may need numerous encounters during immersion before they make it into your long-term memory.

The second purpose of this exercise is to train yourself to say these words with correct pronunciation and phonetic stress automatically. Take this time to work on reducing your accent as you say aloud new words that you are learning. Pay special attention to properly producing each sound like a native speaker would. This special attention makes all the difference in building an authentic Spanish accent.

For example, when you see "to test" on the front side of this flashcard exercise, instead of just quickly muttering "probar", say it aloud with proper pronunciation. Really focus on the tapped 'R's to make your "probar" sound native.

Short and Sweet

What if you reverse the order and put Spanish on the front and English on the back? This would change the Production exercise to a reading and translation exercise, which is useful, yet you will get plenty of reading from the Cloze and Shadowing exercises. Additionally, the Listening exercises will give you a more interesting way to test your recognition of these words.

Putting just the English word on the front side of this flashcard saves a lot of time, or as an alternative, you could also put an image representing the word here and exclude English altogether. The choice is yours. An appropriate image can be found for most words, but abstract words like "tibio" (lukewarm) and "distracción" (distraction) will be much more difficult to find clear and unambiguous images for. In some cases, the English word might be the easiest option.

It's highly recommended to stick with just single words and small phrases. If you put full English sentences on the front and try to recall them verbatim in Spanish, you can potentially put yourself through language learning hell. The possibility of all kinds of synonyms and plausible translations makes it frustrating. Too many questions can come up when you think of an answer that seems correct yet is different from the answer on the back. You might find yourself irritated wondering whether the answer that you came up with in your head is correct or not. It's tedious and not a very pleasant learning experience.

Let's say you want to learn from a basic sentence like:

¿Quieres probar un trozo de este pay de manzana?

Would you like to try a bit of this apple pie?

Instead of trying to memorize the full sentence, use these basic Production exercises to practice any potentially new words like the following:

- probar (to test)

- un trozo (a piece / a bit)

- manzana (apple)

- pay (pie).

Or make exercises for very short phrases like:

- este pay de manzana (this apple pie)

- ¿Quieres probar? (Do you want to test?).

Cloze

If you are a fan of learning through context, Cloze is the exercise for you. And it can be used to learn more than just isolated vocabulary and short phrases.

On the front side of these cards, you will be presented with a small context (a sentence or a few sentences) that you have learned beforehand except that one small piece will be missing. The objective is to figure out what is missing using the surrounding context and then write the answer in your notebook. That missing piece can be a vocabulary word, a piece of grammar, a part of a phrase, or even a verb conjugation. This simple exercise will require you to think in Spanish while strengthening your reading and writing skills with virtually no stress.

Context is what makes these exercises interesting and fun. Test for the right vocabulary in context. Test and learn any phrase one word at a time. Test for those tricky Spanish verb conjugations in context (present, preterite, imperfect, conditional, future). Test for the correct grammar particle which can seem so oddly specific at times. This includes pronouns in Spanish (e.g. me, te, el, la, los, las, lo, le, les, os, and nos) which some people struggle with. To summarize, if something is new or still unfamiliar to you in a sentence, make it a Cloze card.

There is no need to write any word more than once. There is no need to test for large amounts of missing information. There is no need to copy whole sentences down in your notebook. There is no need to memorize these sentences to recite later.

Instead, you will see all of the new words, grammar particles, and verb conjugations again and again in the variety of Anki cards that you can make for each context that you choose from your coursebook and selected native materials. And while you are testing yourself on something small, you will still need to use the other information to help you determine the missing piece.

Of course you can also use Production exercises to test verb conjugations as well as the gender of nouns, but Cloze exercises offer a potentially stronger means to practice grammar through context. And they get you to actively read and write the foreign language. While there is no substitute for reading native Spanish, these exercises offer a supplement that can also help build reading comprehension early on. They are helpful for language pattern recognition, sentence building, and even spelling.

It may sound like a silly and over-simplified elementary school exercise, but it's a highly effective strategy to help you learn any potentially confusing language concept one word at a time. Remove just "por" or "para" from sentences and practice figuring out which one should be used. The same goes for "ser" vs "estar" and other initially difficult language structures.

Learn new expressions like "no tener pelos en la lengua" (to tell it like it is) one word at a time. Make cards for even the easy vocabulary you are very familiar with that are found within these new expressions and phrases. It's an easy way to internalize longer bits of language. Even lengthy and challenging passages and paragraphs can be broken up, practiced, and conquered one word at a time.

We strongly recommend resisting the temptation to test more than one word at a time. Imagine that you wanted to learn a new expression or phrase like "no tener pelos en la lengua", and you created a single Cloze card where two or three of these words were missing. When several words are absent, there is much less context to work with. Even when just two or three words are missing from a lengthy sentence, there might not always be enough context to be able to figure out exactly what is missing. It creates an unnecessary level of difficulty that can lead to a gradual build up of frustration. To avoid this frustration, test only word at a time.

To create Cloze cards in Anki, first make sure 'Cloze' is selected at the top left corner when adding cards. Now, place your text in the 'Front' box. Next, highlight the single word that you wish to practice and press the "[...]" button. Click 'Add', and you are all finished.

Listening

The Listening exercises are simply listening more or less, but Text to Speech programs can completely change how we practice foreign listening comprehension these days. There exists a way to take words, phrases, and sentences from any source of Spanish and generate free audio recordings of an automated native speaker saying those words. These audio recordings can then be placed inside of Anki to make listening the easiest and most fun language skill to practice.

The front side to these flashcard exercises will be blank, but an audio file of roughly two to three seconds in Spanish will play. It's your task to either think or say aloud the equivalent in your native tongue. You either get it or don't within three seconds. It's a very simple and effective exercise in training your ears to instantly decode the meaning of spoken words just like you can in your first language. The Cloze exercises do take a little time and effort to figure out, but the Listening and Production cards help break up the monotony with on the spot lightning round challenges.

On the back side of these flashcard exercises, we recommend putting the English translation and the Spanish transcription of the audio file to check for complete comprehension. Cloze and potentially Production can be done in only Spanish, but using

English here is perhaps the fastest way to check if you fully understand the meaning behind the words.

Unlike the Production cards, however, you can test your comprehension of both single words and full sentences one by one. Undoubtedly, there are going to be some synonyms when translating full sentences from one language to another, but it takes much less effort to translate sentences from the target language to our native language. Try it yourself and see how fast they go by.

Shadowing

We will admit that this last exercise requires a few hoops to jump through to setup inside of Anki. We understand that you may not be willing to acquire source files and extract audio from them. If it is too much of a hassle, you can skip this exercise. It is optional.

The Shadowing technique is one way to put more Spanish on our tongues. It was developed and popularized by hyperpolyglot Alexander Arguelles, and in its original form, it requires long dialogues and short stories as well as adequate space to march back and forth in. We would like to include a somewhat condensed form of Shadowing that can be done sitting at the computer using Anki.

It's as simple as repeating aloud what you are hearing as you hear it to the best of your ability. In Shadowing, you do not repeat after the audio, but instead, you talk on top of it continuously for the entire recording. Just one or two attempts each time will be good enough.

There are three types of Shadowing that can be done: Shadowing with no text (Blind Shadowing), Shadowing with the English translation, and Shadowing with the transcription in the foreign language. All of them will include audio in the foreign language of course. To create these exercises in Anki, simply just place the text and audio in the 'Front' box and leave the 'Back' box empty.

When no text is present, you are focusing solely on the sounds of the language and reproducing them with your mouth as best as you can. Even though you may have little to no idea what you are saying, the point is to listen intensively and get used to the feeling of speaking new sounds and words.

When Shadowing with the English translation, you are still repeating what you hear but now with complete understanding. Don't worry about the exact meaning of each word or the structure of the sentences but instead just focus on the overall meaning here.

And when Shadowing with the Spanish transcription, you are listening, speaking, and reading in Spanish all at once. Use the text to help you pronounce all the words while still focusing on copying the native speaker's intonation and rhythm.

Shadowing can feel like quite the workout, as it can quickly fatigue the muscles in your mouth which have to work double time in order to keep up with the native speaker. But if you are interested in things like proper intonation and pronunciation, speaking confidence, and accent reduction, this is the technique for you. It's also fairly challenging and incredibly fun.

Unfortunately, this exercise can only be done with video and audio sources of Spanish, so written materials will be left out. There are methods to get native speakers to record such lines, but they are highly inconvenient and generally not worth the time and money to acquire. Also, text-to-speech robots are not yet accurate enough to imitate natural intonation, so we do not recommend Shadowing after them.

How to Setup

When you download, install, and open up Anki, click 'Create Deck' and name it whatever you like. You will only need one deck for now, as all four of the flashcard types will go into this deck. Click 'Add' at the top and then click 'Basic' at the top of the new window. By default, you should see four card types.

THE ORIGINAL FOUR CARD TYPES IN ANKI

Let's add Production, Listening, and Shadowing cards. Creating card types for each one takes seconds and allows for easy reference and organization if you ever wish to change something in bulk. If you click "Manage", you can delete the unnecessary cards but keep "Cloze". Next, click "Add" and select "Add:Basic" and rename it to "Production". Repeat this process for "Listening" and "Shadowing."

After that, you will need to install an add-on called "AwesomeTTS" (*https://ankiweb.net/shared/info/301952613*). It offers multiple free Text to Speech services that you can integrate into Anki. With a simple install and Anki reboot, you can simply paste a word or sentence into the 'Front' or 'Back' box, highlight it, and click the new speaker icon from the add-on to quickly generate the audio in seconds.

At the time of writing this book, AwesomeTTS only works with Anki 2.0 versions and not the newer versions. Fortunately, you can find still find the 2.0 version on Anki's main website page.

AwesomeTTS will allow you to do the Listening and Shadowing card types by placing these files into the 'Front' box. You can also add extra audio reinforcement to your Production and Cloze cards by placing these files in the 'Back' box. When these exercises appear during Anki review sessions, the sound file will automatically play by default, but you can replay the sound file when needed by pressing the 'R' button on your keyboard.

Finally, the cards are reviewed in the order that they are made by default, but shuffling the cards is strongly recommended. Otherwise, the same words and contexts will be clumped together in consecutive exercises, and after the first card, you will simply be testing your short-term memory rather than your long-term memory.

To shuffle the cards, open Anki and click on the gear to the right of your deck and select 'Options'. Click the 'New cards' tab, look for 'Order', and select 'Show new cards in random order'. And if there is ever a time you would like to reshuffle the deck for whatever reason, select 'Show new cards in order added', press OK, select 'Show new cards in random order' again, and press OK again.

Inserting Images and Audio

Images and audio from instructional and native materials aren't required, but they are a means to create a stronger link from what you are reviewing inside Anki to what you are reading and listening to every day. The original image and audio can make

Anki sessions much more meaningful and memorable, and your efforts here will be rewarded.

For instance, still images from videos are super easy to insert. While the video is on the screen and paused at the appropriate moment, press the 'PrtSc' button (Command + Shift + 3 for Macs) on your keyboard. Then, you will need to open up a basic image editing program like Paint in Windows (Paintbrush for Macs) and crop the image to your liking before saving it. When adding cards to Anki, make sure the cursor is in the 'Front' text box and then click the paperclip icon to add your image or audio.

Coursebooks and textbooks provide easy access to native speaker recordings via CD, but inserting audio from native materials is a little more difficult. For educational purposes, you will need to obtain the original audio or video source.

There are of course many ways to create the audio clips you want. We found the free audio editing program Audacity (*http://www.audacityteam.org*) to work well enough in the past.

Example Passage

To demonstrate these exercises in action, let's look at a basic example sentence, break it down, and see what exercises we can create to master any potentially new language here.

<u>Sample Context:</u>
La casa del protagonista se encuentra en una zona tranquila.

<u>Translation:</u>
The protagonist's house is located in a peaceful area.

Quick Breakdown:

- La casa (the house)

- del (of the)

- protagonista (protagonist)

- se encuentra (is located)

- en (in)

- una zona (a zone)

- tranquila (peaceful).

Anki Practice Exercises:

Here's just one out of many possible combinations of Anki exercises that you could make for these sentences:

protagonist

Production # 1: el protagonista

to be (located)

Production # 2: encontrarse

calm / quiet / peaceful

Production # 3: tranquilo(a)

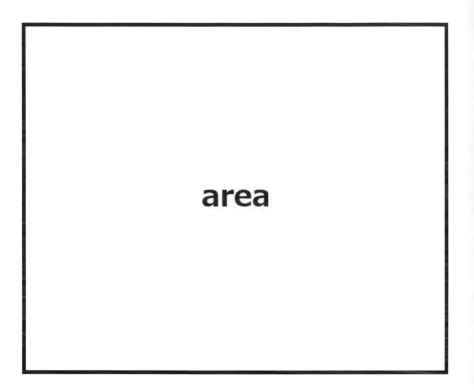

Production # 4: la zona

La casa[...]protagonista se encuentra en una zona tranquila.

Cloze # 1: del

La casa del protagonista

[...]encuentra en

una zona tranquila.

Cloze # 2: se

La casa del protagonista

se   [...]   en

una zona tranquila.

Cloze # 3: encuentra

La casa del protagonista

se encuentra en

una zona   [...]   .

Cloze # 4: tranquila

el protagonista

(audio file)

Listening # 1: the protagonist

encontrarse

(audio file)

Listening # 2: to be located

tranquila

(audio file)

Listening # 3: calm / quiet / peaceful

la zona

(audio file)

Listening # 4: the area

(image and audio only)

Shadowing # 1: with no text

The protagonist's house is located in a peaceful area.

Shadowing # 2: with English translation

La casa del protagonista se encuentra en una zona tranquila.

Shadowing # 3: with Spanish transcription

Divide and Conquer

Ultimately, you may use the Anki exercises any way that you wish, but here is one way to dissect new native material. New words and phrases get one Production and one Listening card. Cloze cards can also be used for some of these words and phrases if additional practice is desired. Otherwise, new or still unfamiliar grammar structures and verb conjugations get one Cloze card. Shadowing gets three cards (Blind Shadowing, Shadowing with English text, and Shadowing with Spanish text).

And here are some possible ways you could apply these Anki exercises to master your initial Spanish coursebook. For new vocabulary words and set phrases, create one Production and one Listening card. For every major grammar point or topic covered, grab three, four, or five sentences and make one Listening card for each. You can use Cloze cards here as well to test for vocabulary and correct grammar usage if you think there is enough context to make the answer clear and unambiguous.

Verb conjugation tables can be tackled with Production and Listening exercises. There is no need to make these cards for every possible conjugation and verb however. These exercises are to build a basic intuition on how verbs function in Spanish and not to memorize every single conjugation. Knowing every conjugation near-perfectly is a task best left to extensive reading and listening.

For now, start with Production and Listening exercises for just three, four, or five verbs. Focus only on the most basic tenses at first like the present, preterite, and imperfect tenses. Rather than make one Production and one Listening card for every conjugation (yo, tú, él/ella/usted, nosotros, vosotros, ellos/ellas/ustedes), split the conjugations between the two exercises to save time. You can always make more as you learn new verbs and verb tenses.

Monologues, dialogues, and long passages found in textbooks are perfect for Cloze as well as Shadowing exercises. These scenarios provide good opportunities to speak alongside a native speaker and to try to keep up with their intonation and speed to the best of your ability. Use Production, Cloze, and Listening as you see fit to breakdown all the new vocabulary, phrases, and grammar in these larger contexts. The Shadowing cards may be few and far in between during review sessions, but you can use these gigantic gaps to gauge your personal progress as you eventually encounter each one.

A high amount of Production and Listening, a moderate amount of Cloze, and a low amount of Shadowing has worked well for us in the past, but feel free to experiment with this ratio.

SPEEDING UP THE PROCESS

Back in Chapter Three, we covered how you can start learning Spanish by reading and listening to native materials starting from day one but with a somewhat heavier emphasis on listening over reading. After all, reading in a foreign language can be so overwhelmingly difficult at first, and listening to the foreign language is just much more beginner-friendly in comparison.

But if you're using the Spanish subtitles to learn from things like TV shows and YouTube videos, you are learning Spanish not only through listening but reading as well. Reading does not always have to mean reading from dusty, old books. In fact, it can be done in all sorts of non-traditional ways like when we use Spanish subtitles to learn specific lines and moments from shows we are watching. And it can be even more useful when done in larger quantities.

The challenge lies in figuring out how to get yourself to read more Spanish every day. This final chapter will focus on why you should read more Spanish every day and techniques you can use to ease into extensive reading and also extensive listening.

After studying comes to an end for the day, why read when you can listen for hours on end? For starters, it will help you to quickly convert more of that incomprehensible stream of Spanish gibberish into a language you can understand. Secondly, it provides another fun and holistic way keep engaged in learning and ultimately living through Spanish for hours every day. Third, some of the world's most skilled polyglots like Alexander Arguelles, Luca

Lampariello, and Steve Kaufmann are major advocates of reading as a means to learn foreign languages. And finally and most importantly, extensive reading is perhaps one the most effective ways to build and easily maintain a massive range of vocabulary in a foreign language.

Reading native Spanish materials can be tremendously slow and difficult as a beginner, so when exactly should you start reading things other than Spanish subtitles? As soon as possible is ideal if you're looking to get really good at Spanish within a few years. The more you expose yourself to written Spanish the better. The more early attempts at reading you make, the faster you will learn.

So let's say you did decide to do some extensive reading, for example, by playing a video game in Spanish. Do you always stop to look up every unfamiliar word the entire game? When do you just relax and play the game? Handling such a large amount of text in any foreign language can be completely overwhelming at first, and you can be left completely drained and discouraged after just a day or two. This is where smart language learning strategies can come in handy.

Intensive vs. Extensive Reading

To answer these questions, we need to understand the difference between intensive and extensive reading. In intensive reading, the goal is to break down and look up every single new word and grammar point in a selected text of relatively short length. Information learned here can be reviewed through tools like Anki and the Goldlist Method. This kind of reading is only intended to last around 20-45 minutes. The techniques described back in Chapter Three are examples of intensive reading and listening.

In extensive reading, however, the goal is to read for pleasure and for longer periods of time. And unlike intensive reading, no effort should be made to review information through Anki and other means. You can only study a small amount of pages of a difficult text before your mind starts giving out, but when you read a text that is easy for your level, you can read a much larger quantity of pages for several hours with only a few breaks in between.

Unfortunately, the problem is that it's very tough to find extensive reading materials for your level when you are in the beginner and intermediate stages. It's estimated that you need 98% comprehension of a text before you are able to do true extensive reading.

Ideally, you're supposed to rely on mostly context alone to learn new words in extensive reading. But in reality, no matter what material you choose to start with, there will be a ton of words that you have never seen or heard before. It's very likely that you will have to go through your first reading material heavily with a dictionary or English translation in order to understand what's happening in the text.

Just like how there's no magical point where you're ready for native Spanish materials, there's also no magical point where you're ready for extensive reading. In order to successfully bridge the gap between intensive reading and extensive reading, a long series of efforts at reading must be made. There are principles of extensive reading, however, that you can use at any level to make this process much more enjoyable and faster overall.

The first step is to be absolutely clear whether you are doing intensive reading or extensive reading. By all means, continue to do the intensive reading and listening activity discussed back in Chapter Three, as it can be quite useful at any level. Although when you feel ready to try something new, extensive reading is here to help speed up the rate at which you progress towards fluency.

Limiting Anki Reviews

The next step is to make sure you actually have enough time to read by making a few small adjustments to Anki's schedule so that you aren't stuck reviewing cards for more than two hours every day. Regardless of how much time you can devote every day towards learning Spanish, lengthy Anki review sessions are completely unnecessary. There comes a point where your time is much better spent doing things like extensive reading.

Anki review sessions involve doing new cards (color coded blue in Anki) and review cards (color coded green in Anki). New cards are exercises that have been created but not yet seen during review sessions. Review cards have been viewed at least once before. So an Anki session with 10 new cards and 10 review cards will be referred to here as a 10/10 session, which would be 20 exercises altogether.

In Anki, you can set the number of exercises to be completed per day to 10/10 or to whatever numbers you would like. This can easily be done by opening Anki, clicking on the gear to the right of your deck, and selecting 'Options'. Set 'New cards/day' to 10, and then click the 'Reviews' tab and set 'Maximum reviews/day' to 10.

Our starting recommendation is set at 10/10 review sessions, and caution is advised if you would like to increase those numbers. If you want to incorporate more Anki reviews, a larger number such as 20/20 could potentially be done if broken into two or more smaller sessions throughout the day. Doing such a large number every day will be a tremendously difficult habit to maintain, but if you are feeling particularly motivated to do more Anki on certain days, go for it.

100 "Maximum reviews/day" is the current default setting in Anki at the time of writing this book, but if you keep this setting, Anki review sessions alone can quickly start exceeding 90 minutes daily when the reviews begin to pile up. This does not include the time it takes to create cards from new material let alone read and listen to it.

Doing a needlessly high amount of Anki cards day after day can be more detrimental than helpful. More Anki does not mean more learning and progress if it causes your internal motivation meter to plummet and approach zero. There's no need to train for the Agony Olympics with hellishly long ultra-marathons of Anki reviews.

You can do exponentially more Anki cards in the long-term by avoiding burnout just by doing small sessions consistently as a habit. To build this consistency with Anki, keep sessions under an hour and don't force yourself to do more for the sake of faster progress. Stop right before you get bored and keep yourself hungry for the next session.

If you have trouble focusing during 10/10 sessions, start with 5/5 sessions. Train to grow stronger in both your Spanish proficiency and ability to deeply focus. If you have a habit of waking up and going straight to social media in the morning, chances are that you will have great difficulty in trying to maintain focus while studying or reading and listening to raw Spanish.

You might find that you have more focus and energy when you start your day with things like morning walks, meditation, inspirational audiobooks, and exercise. Their importance should not be underestimated in the slightest. How you start your day can determine whether your time and energy will be sapped by all the distractions of the world or will be channeled 100% into doing the things that matter the most to you.

Principles of Extensive Reading

Now that you have enough time available to start extensive reading, let's take a look at five principles to help make reading a much more pleasurable and overall effective learning experience. The more pleasurable it is the more time you'll naturally want to spend doing it which equates to you learning faster.

Perhaps the biggest improvement you can make to your reading comprehension and speed is to read silently. While reading aloud can certainly be beneficial to pronunciation, it is a telltale sign of intensive reading. But in extensive reading, it's completely unnecessary for the most part. Continuously reading aloud makes reading painfully slow and unnatural which in fact pushes you further away from extensive reading.

Think about reading in your native language. Have you been reading this chapter aloud? Have you been moving your lips to form the words with your mouth? If English is your native language, the answer to these questions is most likely no. The reason we can read so well in our native language is not because we practice reading everything aloud. It's because of the massive volume we have read extensively throughout the years, and the overwhelming majority of it was read silently.

For Spanish, try aiming to read silently 95% of the time and save the other five percent for speaking new words aloud with proper pronunciation. In this way, it will be more akin to how you learned to read so well in your native language. You already have more than enough new words to say aloud as a beginner or intermediate learner, and reading aloud anymore than this is just going to slow you down.

The second principle of extensive reading is to read for general meaning, pleasure, and curiosity rather than 100% complete comprehension. In general, once you understand the overall meaning of a sentence, move right along to the next. Don't try to read it aloud or re-read it in at attempt to memorize new vocabulary and grammar structures. These are short-term memory tactics that have little impact on what is stored in your long-term memory. You naturally learn faster when you allow yourself to naturally read. Forgetting words means that you are learning them.

Extensive reading is most effective when it is the means to an end and not the other way around. The end goal in mind should be the content you're really interested in. And when Spanish is the means to that end, you get really good at the language as a result through the sheer volume of comprehensible input you receive through reading.

Our third principle of extensive reading is to find something to read that is not the news. Reading the news from time to time can be quite beneficial in learning the geography, politics, and current events of Spanish speaking countries, but you may not find this information compelling enough to do it extensively.

It's very typical of Spanish learners and language learners in general to try to read the news in the target language, as it seems like a reasonable and logical goal to aim towards. Yet the truth is that it can be tremendously hard to stay consistent in reading these types of traditional reading materials every day. After a few weeks or months, it can seem like an endless stream of Spanish to work through. This is because news articles aren't connected most of the time. There's no overarching story driving you to read until the very end to find out what happens.

That drive you get from a great story is what compels you to continue reading through the most difficult moments. This is why we highly recommend reading any and all kinds of fictional stories from start to finish. This could be anything from short stories, popular novels like *Harry Potter*, or even stories told through video games. And if you aren't a fan of physical books or video games, you could even start extensive reading by going through a TV show or movie line by line using the Spanish subtitles. Of course, non-fiction can work just as well if you have a particular topic that fascinates you like European history as an example.

If you are looking for some fictional stories to start with for free, try reading *Alice in Wonderland* which you can find in a bilingual text format at Bilinguis (*http://bilinguis.com/book/alice/es/en*). If you have never read *Don Quixote de la Mancha* before, make it a goal to read this classic Spanish novel in its original language which you can find for free at Loyal Books (*http://www.loyalbooks.com/book/don-quijote-vol-1-by-miguel-de-cervantes-saavedra*). This site also offers an audiobook version for free that can be listened to anywhere and at anytime after reading to help reinforce all the new language you encounter.

If you are easily distracted while at the computer, however, you may have more success with a physical copy of a book or at a least printed copy of some reading material found online. At first, it might seem unnecessary to take the extra time and money to acquire physical copies when almost everything is immediately available through the internet. But what you gain in exchange is very much worth the effort. Not only is it a terrific feeling to hold actual books in a foreign language in your hands, you can also be at your highest level of concentration while working your way through. Flipping through real pages is all the more satisfying and beats clicking through internet pages anytime.

The fourth principle we would like to introduce is to use bilingual texts whenever possible. Of course, the dictionary is useful at any level in figuring out the meaning to new words, but having a copy of the text translated in your native language can drastically increase your reading speed. Reading in new languages is an incredible amount of work in the beginning, and you will want every advantage you can get to speed up the process.

Translations can help you focus on getting to the next part of the story rather than trying to comprehend the Spanish text 100%. When you read the translation of the text in your native language, you instantly comprehend the meaning of the text 100% and are ready to continue forward. This can help prevent you from getting hung up on why certain language was used in the Spanish text. As long as you are engaging the target language in the text and trying to understand it before reading the translation, it does not matter how often you use the English text even if it's initially sentence by sentence.

The fifth and final principle of extensive reading is to track your progress using a notebook. It is by no means required just like bi-lingual texts, but keeping a written log of how much you read every day is like magic in helping you build confidence in your reading ability. These feelings of improvement and growth are the foundation of a long-term habit of extensive reading. It will give you a deep sense of accomplishment each day to see how much progress you made and to compare it with how much you have made on previous days. That tingly and fuzzy feeling you will receive makes it all the easier to come back the next day and chip away at whatever material you're reading through.

Use each page, chapter, short story, written article, and whatever means you can to track your reading speed and progress. Obviously printed materials are going to be much more straightforward to track using pages, but sometimes you have to be a bit creative. For instance, even if you decide to first practice extensive reading using the Spanish subtitles to a TV show, it's very much worth keeping a record of how many minutes of video time you clear each day. Any record at all can make your growth and process both tangible and visible.

Extensive Listening

Extensive listening, on the other hand, is as simple as picking something to watch and pressing play. That's it. There's no need to listen for the high frequency words here. You just listen purely for pleasure. Ideal extensive listening times include but are not limited to when you are in need of a break from reading or when you are tired at the end of the day.

Binge watching is highly encouraged! More listening equals higher comprehension skills, and you will even learn a thing or two intermittently through context alone. The parts you can't understand help motivate you to come back the next day ready to learn more.

The real test lies in deciding to follow more Spanish shows than you follow in English. This habit of immersing yourself in native Spanish should take precedence over your old hobbies if you really want to reach an advanced or even near-native level within a few years. You need to train your eyes and ears daily and put in every hour and minute that you can.

Choosing which old hobbies and activities to sacrifice to make time for more Spanish is a difficult choice, but it's much easier to start with the dead times of the day or what is also known as downtime. Turn this downtime into "uptime" by taking a book to read wherever you go. Time spent walking, biking, and driving can be turned into listening time by making sure your mobile device is always stocked with hours of Spanish entertainment to listen to.

Going complete immersion in your home environment is not required for fluency, but either way you'll see significantly more satisfying results when you start living primarily through Spanish.

Experiment by making your own Spanish schedules to suit your personal needs. You could start the day with Anki and intensive reading and listening first and move on to extensive reading and listening later. You could even try switching between intensive and extensive activities to give yourself a break when needed. Or you could go straight into only extensive reading and listening. Test your own ideas and see what brings the most learning and enjoyment to your journey.

Lang-8, Italki, and HelloTalk

Output practice could also fill in for some of this time in your schedule. Let's look at three different ways to get in contact with native speakers and receive corrections.

Lang-8 (*http://lang-8.com*) is a free language exchange website where users make posts in the language that they wish to practice. Users can write just about anything and everything. You can write about what has been on your mind all day or even specific topics that you are interested in. You receive corrections in exchange for correcting other people's posts in your native language.

In terms of time and money, Lang-8 may be the most effective way of receiving corrections. It is very convenient to visit the page at any time, write for 10-20 minutes, make a few easy corrections for other users, and leave to go about your day. The next day or even later during the same day, you can return to Lang-8 to find corrections to your post.

If you are willing to pay a few dollars a session to speak with tutors face to face, Italki (*https://www.italki.com*) may be the better alternative. In order to use Italki, you will need to search for a teacher of your liking, schedule for an available time slot, and log on to Skype (*https://www.skype.com*) just before the arranged time. Face-to-face conversation and tutoring does have its advantages, so it may be worth the price to you.

HelloTalk (*https://www.hellotalk.com*) is a highly popular app that has opened new possibilities for language exchange through texting. Most language learners rate this app very positively, as it is possibly the most convenient way to connect directly with native speakers of almost any language. It's a great platform to start organic conversations with people from different countries across the world. Make new friends as you talk in each other's native language and also give and receive corrections along the way. Texting certainly takes the pressure off of face to face conversations in meeting new people, so this may be the choice for you.

Living the Language

Anki is great in the beginner and early intermediate stages for internalizing the basics of Spanish, but in the end, it's not the most efficient when it comes to building vocabulary and overall language competency. If you try putting every new word you learn into Anki, it will slow down your reading and listening to a snail's pace. And even if you were to do just an hour of Anki reviews every day at the mid to late intermediate levels, it can be infinitely more fun to spend that hour reviewing those thousands of words through more reading and listening to native Spanish or even communicating with native speakers.

You get really good not by studying a few hundred pages but by reading thousands of pages. That's how you win the game. When you finally stop studying and reviewing in favor of extensive reading and listening, you start to feel that you're not just learning the language anymore but you're truly living it.

After reading thousands of pages and listening to countless hours of Spanish, you will have seen and heard just about everything. You'll come to understand everything almost instantly like native speakers do. And Spanish will come just as natural to your tongue as your native language does. At that point, you might even be tempted to learn another language and become a polyglot yourself.

Made in the USA
Columbia, SC
09 June 2019